Sloths

Victoria Blakemore

Table of Contents

What Are Sloths?

Sloths are the slowest moving kind of mammal.

There are two main kinds of sloths: two-toed sloths and three-toed sloths.

In the wild, sloths usually live
between ten and twenty years.

Blending in

Sloths are gray and brown, but can look green. They move so slowly that **algae** can grow on their fur!

The algae helps the sloths by working as a **camouflage** so the sloths blend in with trees.

Physical Characteristics

Sloth fur grows in the opposite direction from most animals.

This helps sloths because they spend much of their time upside down and it lets water run off of their fur.

Sloth fur grows away from their
stomach.

Habitat

Sloths live in rainforests where the weather is warm and there are lots of trees.

They spend most of their time in the trees so they are safe from **predators**.

Sloths need tall trees to stay safe from predators like jaguars.

Range

Sloths are only found in the rainforests of Central and South America.

Many sloths live in Costa Rica,

Peru, Venezuela, Colombia,

and Brazil

Diet

Most sloths are **herbivores**, which means that they only eat plants. They eat tree leaves, flowers, and shoots.

Sloths need to drink very little water because most of the water they get comes from the plants they eat.

Some sloths are **omnivores**.

They eat insects as well as

plants.

Communication

Sloths often make a hissing

sound, but they are also able

to squeal and grunt.

They make a low cry when

they are in danger.

Scent

Sloths also use scent to communicate with other sloths. They have a special scent gland they use for marking their **territory**. This tells other sloths that the area is taken.

Sloths have an excellent sense

of smell.

Movement

Sloths are great climbers. Their claws are long and curved, which lets them hang upside down for long periods of time. They can even sleep upside down!

Sloth claws are perfect for

gripping tree branches.

On the Ground

While they are helpful for climbing, a sloth's claws make it impossible for them to stand up. They have to crawl when they are on the ground.

Sloths spend most of their time in trees because they are too slow on the ground to get away from predators.

Baby Sloths

Female sloths have one
baby. Babies are born with
their fur and claws.

The mother takes care of
the baby for between six
and nine months.

The baby rides on the mother's back or stomach for up to five weeks.

Solitary Animals

Sloths are solitary animals, which means that they spend most of their time alone.

Sloths have very little energy because of the food they eat, so they end up sleeping a lot. They can sleep up to 18 hours each day!

Sloths spend a lot of their

time sleeping in the trees.

Pygmy Three-Toed Sloths

The pygmy three-toed sloth is **endangered**. There are not many left in the wild.

They are found only in the red mangrove forests of an island off the coast of Panama. They are known for being very good swimmers.

The pygmy three-toed sloth is
facing habitat loss.

Sloths in Danger

Sloth habitats are being destroyed and some sloth species are in danger of **extinction.**

Roads also pose a danger to sloths who are on the ground.

Sloths are too slow to move
out of the way of cars when
they are crossing the road.

Helping Sloths

Places like the Sloth

Sanctuary in Costa Rica

are working to help sloths.

They rescue sloths that are

sick or hurt. They take care

of the sloths until they are

well enough to go back to

their habitat.

There are also people who
stop their cars and help
sloths cross the street.

Giant Sloths

People have found fossils of
sloths that were as big as
elephants!

Scientists think that these
giant sloths used to live on
the ground.

Ground sloths, or **Milodons**,

became **extinct** thousands of

years ago.

Glossary

Algae: a plant-like organism that grows in wet habitats

Camouflage: an animal's way of hiding by blending in with the surroundings

Endangered: at risk of becoming extinct

Extinct: no longer alive

Extinction: when an entire species is no longer living

Herbivore: an animal that eats

only plants

Milodons: large sloths that lived

on the ground thousands of years

ago

Omnivore: an animal that eats

plants and other animals

Predator: an animal that hunts

other animals for food

Stable: steady, unchanging

Territory: an area of land that an

animal claims as its own

Victoria Blakemore is a first grade

teacher in Southwest Florida with a

passion for reading.

You can visit her at

www.elementaryexplorers.com

Also in This Series

Also in This Series

Aardvarks · Mako Sharks · Alligators · Frogs · Hedgehogs · Brown Bears · Bongos

Sea Turtles · Quokkas · Muskrats · Zebras · Red Foxes · Ring-Tailed Lemurs · Platypuses

Anteaters · Kangaroos · Rhinos · Jaguars · Wombats · Capybaras · Gorillas

Cats · Skunks · Butterflies · Dingoes · Snow Leopards · African Wild Dogs · Penguins

Whale Sharks · Wolverines · Warthogs · Caracals · Badgers · Seals · Hummingbirds

Pikas · Humpback Whales · Pumas · Lemonade · Llamas · Tulips · Ostriches

Sunflowers · Fennec Foxes

Printed in the USA
CPSIA information can be obtained
at www.ICGtesting.com
LVHW071926011124
795435LV00047B/1192

9 780998 824345